John Calvin

by Simonetta Carr

with Illustrations by Emanuele Taglietti

REFORMATION HERITAGE BOOKS

Grand Rapids, Michigan

John Calvin
© 2008 by Simonetta Carr

Cover artwork by Emanuele Taglietti: John Calvin at his desk writing *The Institutes of the Christian Religion.* For additional artwork by Emanuele, see pages 9, 12, 14, 17, 18, 21, 22, 25, 26, 29, 34, 37, 41, 46, 50, 53, and 54. © 2008 by Emanuele Taglietti

Published by
Reformation Heritage Books
2965 Leonard St. NE
Grand Rapids, MI 49525
616-977-0889 / Fax: 616-285-3246
e-mail: orders@heritagebooks.org
website: www.heritagebooks.org

Library of Congress Cataloging-in-Publication Data

Carr, Simonetta.
 John Calvin / by Simonetta Carr ; with illustrations by Emanuele Taglietti.
     p. cm. — (Christian biographies for young readers)
  ISBN 978-1-60178-055-3 (hardcover : alk. paper)
 1. Calvin, Jean, 1509-1564—Juvenile literature. 2. Reformation—Switzerland—Geneva—Biography—Juvenile literature. I. Taglietti, Emanuele. II. Title.
  BX9418.C39 2008
  284'.2092—dc22
  [B]
                                            2008048249

For additional Reformed literature, request a free book list from Reformation Heritage Books at the above address.

Printed in the United States of America
17 18 19 20 21/11 10 9 8 7 6 5

CHRISTIAN BIOGRAPHIES FOR YOUNG READERS

This series introduces children to important people in the Christian tradition. Parents and school teachers alike will welcome the excellent educational value it provides for students, while the quality of the publication and the artwork make each volume a keepsake for generations to come. Furthermore, the books in the series go beyond the simple story of someone's life by teaching young readers the historical and theological relevance of each character.

AVAILABLE VOLUMES OF THE SERIES

John Calvin
Augustine of Hippo
John Owen
Athanasius
Lady Jane Grey
Anselm of Canterbury
John Knox
Jonathan Edwards
Marie Durand
Martin Luther
Peter Martyr Vermigli
Irenaeus of Lyon

Acknowledgments

Thanks to my children, Christian, Simon, Dustin, David, Jonathan, Kevin, Raphael, and Renaissance, who have inspired, co-authored, and critiqued this project; to my husband, Tom, for his love and patience; to my mother, Luciana Negrini, for her legacy; to my pastors, Rev. Michael Brown and Dr. Rev. Michael Horton, and to my elder and Westminster Seminary of California graduate Brett Watson, for their help, encouragement, and advice; to my former pastor, Rev. Michael Matossian, Westminster Seminary of California graduate Travis Baker, and my friend Heather Chisholm-Chait, for their meticulous editing of my writing, and to all my church family for their support.

Table of Contents

As you read this book, you can follow John Calvin's travels on this map.

Introduction

John Calvin

During the times described in this book, the Roman Catholic Church had great influence in Europe. The head of that church, the pope, owned a large territory in Italy and fought to protect it. The pope, who called the German nation the "Holy Roman Empire," also appointed the German emperor. Every other nation in Europe feared the pope and tried to keep him as friend. Some individual cities within the empire, however, declared their independence from the Roman Catholic Church.

At a time when the church was more interested in riches and power than in its faithfulness to the teachings of the Bible, some Christians fought to return to the truth. Those who fought for the truth were called "Reformers." To "reform" means "to change for the better" and that period in history is referred to as "the Reformation." John Calvin was one of the most famous Reformers.

CHAPTER ONE

Early Studies

Photo by Marc Ryckaert, Wikimedia Commons

The Cathedral of Noyon. Calvin probably visited it frequently with his father.

John Calvin was born on July 10, 1509, in Noyon, a town in the northern part of France. He was the second of either three or four brothers. His mother, Joan, died when he was still very young. His father, Gerard, worked for the Roman Catholic bishop of Noyon, taking care of legal matters. This job allowed him to give his sons a good education, financed by the church, first through the private tutor of a noble family and later in college.

In those days, children went to college when they were still quite young. John Calvin probably started when he was thirteen or fourteen. He was always an excellent student even when the schools he attended were very strict. At Montaigu College, for example,

Young Calvin at Montaigu College

he had to get up at four o'clock in the morning and study or read all day with almost no time to rest. This taught him to use his time wisely and work hard—something that he did for the rest of his life.

At that time, parents usually decided what their children would do when they grew up. From the start, Gerard thought that his son should become a priest. After John's graduation, however, he suddenly changed his mind. He had come to some disagreements with the bishop and, knowing that lawyers can have a very profitable career, he told John that he should study law instead. Obeying his father, John attended the best schools in the country and received a license to practice law. After Gerard's death, he moved back to Paris to study what he liked best: the ancient languages of the Bible (Hebrew and Greek) and the great writings of the past.

In Paris, John Calvin read the writings of Reformers like Martin Luther, who reminded the church of the original teachings of the Bible: mankind is saved only by grace and only through faith. The Roman Catholic Church, the only established church of that time, taught that in order to be saved, people had to do good works.

Calvin said that it was very difficult for him to disagree with teachings that he had accepted for so long, but he knew that the Bible was the only truth. In his writing he said that it was God who changed his heart and mind, giving him a great "desire to make progress" in the truth he had just found.

The Roman Catholic Church did not like the writings of Luther and other Reformers and it did all it could to stop people from reading and believing them.

Martin Luther (1483–1546)

Calvin leaves Paris disguised as a farmer

In 1533, Nicholas Cop, the head of the University of Paris and a friend of Calvin, gave a speech, which sounded so much like the teachings of Luther that some college and state officers became angry. They did not want these new teachings to be taught openly. Things became so dangerous that Cop had to leave the country.

Some thought that Calvin himself had written the speech, so they went to his college quarters to arrest him, but he was not there. They searched his room and took some of his letters, which identified the names of some of his friends. Calvin knew that it was time for him to move on too, so he left Paris disguised as a farmer.

Calvin spent the next few months in different French cities as a guest of friends, including the king's own sister, Marguerite d'Angouleme, who supported the Reformers.

Francis I finds a poster in his bedroom

Right at that time, a group of French Christians decided to protest against the Roman Catholic Church by making posters describing how the Roman Catholic way of worshiping God was wrong and not based on the Scriptures. When people woke up on the morning of October 18, 1534, the posters were everywhere. There was even one in the king's bedroom!

Obviously, the king, Francis I, was not pleased to find his privacy invaded. More important, he had made an agreement with the Roman Catholic pope and could not risk losing this new and powerful friend. He sent his guards to find the men responsible for the posters.

More than two hundred people were arrested, and twenty killed, including one of Calvin's friends. Calvin decided that it was time to leave France and left on horseback with his roommate and friend, Louis du Tillet.

Taking two servants with them, Calvin and his friend started out to Basel, a university town in what was then called the "Holy Roman Empire," where Nicholas Cop had found refuge. One of these servants, however, did not behave honestly. On their way to Basel, he robbed his masters of all their money and escaped with their best horse. It would have been a total disaster if the other servant had not lent them enough money to make it to Basel and find a place to stay.

Calvin robbed by a servant

Calvin writing the *Institutes*

E. Taglietti

CHAPTER TWO

A Dangerous Faith

Finally, at the end of a long and difficult trip, Calvin arrived in Basel. All he wanted was a quiet corner where he could study and write. There, he heard that many followers of the Reformation were still being burned alive in France and that Francis I allowed it because he believed that their teachings were wrong. Calvin knew that he had to do something about it; otherwise, he said he could have rightly been called a coward and a traitor.

He decided that it was time to publish a book he had already started, entitled *Institutes of the Christian Religion,* to show what Reformers really taught and believed. He dedicated it to Francis I, hoping that maybe he would understand. This book was short and clear. It was then much smaller than the version we have today. As time went by, Calvin kept revising it to make it more accurate and easier to understand. The edition we have now was finally completed when he was fifty years old, just five years before his death. People continue to admire this work as one of the clearest explanations of the Reformed faith. It was quite amazing if we consider that it was his first book of this kind and that he wrote it at the young age of twenty-six! Calvin wanted to teach, but he did not want to become famous, so he usually did not tell others that he was the author. In fact, to be less noticed, he decided to leave Basel, where the book was printed.

After publishing the *Institutes*, Calvin spent some time in Italy as a guest of Renée of France, Duchess of Ferrara. He also returned for a short time to France to take care of all unfinished family business. Because those countries were Roman Catholic and very dangerous for Reformers, he often used different names so he would not be recognized, such as Charles d'Esperville or Martianus Lucianus.

Still looking for some quiet place where he could study and write in peace, he finally decided to move to the city of Strasbourg, on the border of Germany and France. However, because at that time these two countries were at war with each other, he had to take a roundabout way. During this trip, he stopped to rest in Geneva, a beautiful city on a large lake that bordered France.

Geneva was facing many problems at that time. The people there had just declared their independence both from other governments and from the pope, and were trying to work on their own in a town full of disagreements, immorality, and crime. William Farel, the pastor of the local church, was a fiery, redheaded preacher, and not always good at organizing things.

Calvin in Ferrara. The Duchess introduced him as Charles d'Esperville.

Farel told Calvin that if he left Geneva, God would curse his peace.

CHAPTER THREE

Under God's Mighty Hand

Farel had read Calvin's writings and found them very clear and well organized. When he found out that Calvin was spending the night in Geneva, he rushed to invite him to stay and become his fellow-worker.

However, Calvin did not want to stay in Geneva. He was still determined to get to Strasbourg. In fact, he had planned to leave the next day. Then Farel told him that if he left Geneva in that time of great need, just to find some peace, God would curse his peace! Calvin said that he felt as if "God from heaven had laid His mighty hand" on him to stop him from leaving. It was a call that he could not refuse.

Calvin, as you probably remember, was trained in law and accustomed to teaching and writing. In Geneva, however, he found himself working as a pastor and a preacher, organizing a young church in very difficult times. His ideas were not always appreciated because some people were used to doing what they wanted and did not like anyone who told them to change their habits.

Sometimes, when Calvin walked down the street, people mocked him and called him names. Some named their dog "Calvin" to show how much they despised the Reformer.

In spite of that, Calvin kept working to help the church, and even found some time to write a catechism and a confession of faith, in order to give Christians a clear direction to follow.

Some people named their dog "Calvin" to show how much they despised the Reformer.

Many people went to church who never really wanted to be there.

In those days, the church worked closely with the state. Some of the taxes the people paid to the state would be given to the church. In this way, the state assumed it had the authority to insist that everyone go to church. You can imagine there must have been many people who went to church but never really wanted to be there. Sometimes they were so loud during the service—even making rude noises—that the Geneva City Council had to send some police officers to keep order.

Calvin said that the church must have discipline and that people who behaved very badly and did not want to change should not be allowed to take the Lord's Supper. The Geneva City Council agreed with Calvin until they realized that this included some important people.

Then they thought he was going too far. Because Calvin and Farel refused to change their minds, on April 23, 1538, the Geneva City Council told them they had three days to leave Geneva.

Calvin and Farel leaving Geneva

Strasbourg in Calvin's times

CHAPTER FOUR

A Church to Pastor, a Family to Father

In spite of all the problems he had faced in Geneva, Calvin never thought of deserting the job God had given him. Now that he had been sent away, it was difficult to decide what to do next.

Weary and discouraged, Calvin and Farel at first moved to Basel. They had many sad memories in their minds, but Calvin knew that even the worst possible enemies could only do as much as God allows them to do. "Let us humble ourselves," he said, "or we might desire to fight against God when He wants to humble us."

The two friends had planned to stay together, but soon Farel accepted the invitation to be pastor in a nearby Swiss town and, around the same time, Calvin's friend Martin Bucer, another Reformer, invited him to be the pastor of a French-speaking congregation in Strasbourg.

Strasbourg, now in Northern France, was then a free republic with its own government and had become the refuge of many persecuted Christians. After his difficult experience,

Calvin was not sure if he ever wanted to be a pastor again but Bucer used the same argument Farel had used years before: "God will know how to find the rebellious servant, as he found Jonah." Once more, Calvin listened and obeyed.

Calvin's new congregation in Strasbourg was a great encouragement to him. It was made up of faithful Christians who had been persecuted in France yet loved the Lord very much. They all respected the Word and the sacraments.

Calvin lived at first with Martin and Elizabeth Bucer and their six children, and then moved to a small rented house. Being very poor, he took in some students who shared his rent.

Even if Calvin was very busy in Strasbourg, he never forgot the church at Geneva. He wrote several letters to the

Martin Bucer (1491–1551)

believers who were left there to encourage them to stay faithful to God. One day, he received an unexpected letter. The Roman Catholic Cardinal Jacopo Sadoleto had just written the citizens of that town to convince them to return to the Roman Catholic Church. His letter was so well written that the Geneva City Council could not think of a good way to reply. Therefore, they asked Calvin to help.

Calvin answered right away, telling Cardinal Sadoleto that the true church of God was founded on the Bible and not on the traditions of men. His explanation was so clear and effective that the cardinal could not reply.

At that point, most Genevans were convinced that sending Calvin away had been a huge mistake, so they invited him back. Back to Geneva? Calvin was not so sure. When his friend Pierre Viret suggested that Geneva's mild climate might be good for his health, he could not help but think of everything he had suffered there. In fact, he remembered that city as a "cross" and a "place of torture." Genevans repeated their call, and Calvin continued to postpone his answer.

In the meantime, since life was relatively calm for Calvin in Strasbourg, his friends suggested that he should get married. The Roman Catholic Church taught that it was best for ministers of the gospel not to marry, but the Reformers did not find this teaching in the Bible, and thought that a marriage and a family could actually help a believer to practice what the Bible taught.

ANTOINET
BERNARDE
CATHERINE
DAUPHINE
HENRIETTE
JOSETTE
LEOPOLDINE
MADELEINE
MARGOT
NADINE
VIOLE
YVE

In his search for a wife, Calvin did not immediately think of Idelette.

At first, Calvin was not sure if that was the best choice for him, because a Reformer's life in those days seemed much too difficult and dangerous for someone trying to raise a family. Finally, he decided to accept their suggestion and explained what he was looking for: a woman who was pure, not too meticulous, not wasteful, patient, and watchful for his health.

His friends gave him some ideas, but none of their arrangements worked out. At the same time, Calvin was often invited to dinner at the house of a widow, Idelette de Bure. He had started to visit her house while her husband was alive, and the couple had shared with him meals and evening devotions. After the death of her husband, Calvin continued the practice of evening devotions with Idelette and her two children. One of Calvin's friends finally asked him, "What about the gentle Idelette?"

John Calvin and Idelette married in 1540. Marriages in those days were usually more practical than romantic, but Calvin and Idelette loved and appreciated each other very much. His friend William Farel, who had tried to help Calvin in this matter, was pleased that his wife was "upright and honest," and "even pretty."

With Idelette's help, Calvin was able to spend more time working and writing. He spent much time writing commentaries on the Bible, beginning with Paul's letter to the Romans. Other Reformers had already written about that book but he wanted his commentary to be simpler and shorter so that everyone could read it and understand it.

Life was very hard in Calvin's day. Europe was often hit by pestilences like the plague, a terrible sickness that, just two centuries earlier, had killed between a third and two thirds of the continent's population. The same sickness had killed Idelette's first husband. As a pastor, Calvin was constantly faced with illness, poverty, and other very serious problems.

Once, Calvin was called to a prolonged series of meetings in Regensburg, a German town on the Danube River, near the Bavarian forest. The meetings had already started, but Phillip Melanchthon, Luther's right hand man, thought that Calvin should be there.

Calvin traveled by river, which was almost completely frozen at that time. After only a few days in Regensburg, he received news that Strasbourg had been hit by a plague. Two students who had been living in his house had died. Idelette and the children had moved in with some relatives who lived nearby.

Calvin was worried and distressed. He could not leave the meetings, which were going to last a few months. Thinking of his wife and children, he wrote to his friends, "What makes my sorrow grow even more is that I hear that they are in danger, and there is no way that I can help them or, at least, comfort them a little by my presence."

Finally, Calvin returned to find them healthy and safe. However, the plague had left much pain all around them, and there was much work left to do to help and comfort those who had survived.

Calvin reading a sad letter from home

Lake Geneva

CHAPTER FIVE

A Difficult Return

Back from Regensburg, Calvin received more letters from Geneva. The situation was desperate and they really needed his help. His friends kept encouraging him to go. What was he to do? Finally, Farel, with his usual fiery temper, asked him, "Are you waiting for the stones to cry out?"

"Since I remember that I no longer belong to myself, I offer my heart to God as a sacrifice," Calvin finally wrote.

On September 13, 1541, Calvin returned to Geneva, inspired not only by the insistence of the Genevans and of his friends, but also by his great concern for the believers there. The Geneva City Council offered him a salary and a furnished house with a view of Lake Geneva and of the Alps, where he could live with his family.

The new house was always full of guests. Many of them, escaping persecution in other countries, stayed with the Calvins for quite some time.

In Geneva, Calvin went back to preaching as if nothing had happened. He never talked about the problems of the past. On his first day in the pulpit, he started to preach from exactly the same text where he had left off more than three years earlier, when he was asked to leave.

Right away, he worked hard to organize the local church. He believed that churches should be governed according to the Word of God. In just two weeks, he wrote a document called Ecclesiastical Ordinances, with rules, schedules, and explanations of the duties and responsibilities of the church. The church was going to be governed as it was in the days of the New Testament, with pastors, teachers, elders, and deacons. Many churches are keeping the same type of government today.

As a pastor, Calvin preached two sermons every Sunday and sometimes on weekdays, for an average of almost two hundred sermons per year. He also continued writing, teaching, and helping others. The reason why he preached, wrote, and taught so much is that he wanted to strengthen the believers through the Word of God. After many years, the fruit showed in the lives of the people and things became better in Geneva in every way, so much so that the Scottish Reformer John Knox called it "the most perfect school of Christ that ever was on the earth since the days of the apostles."

Calvin started to preach from exactly the same text where he had left off more than three years earlier.

The Geneva Academy

Because so many people wanted to learn more about Reformed Christianity and classical studies (which included the study of Greek, Latin, Hebrew, and philosophy), in 1559 Calvin founded a college called the Geneva Academy, similar to a famous school in Strasbourg where he himself had taught. It was one of the first Protestant colleges in the world. The project took many years to complete but, at one point, the college had more than 1,600 students. Hundreds of them became ministers of the gospel in various countries. Many died as martyrs. Calvin himself was one of the professors of theology there. Since that time, Geneva has been a famous center of studies. In 1872, the Geneva Academy was established as a university.

Students came to Calvin's college from all over Europe. Later, many returned home, taking everything they had learned to their own countries. Some of the men who wrote the catechisms you might learn in Sunday school studied at John Calvin's college.

The first director of Calvin's college was Theodore Beza, a Frenchman who had found refuge in Geneva years before when he was escaping persecution. After spending a few years in Lausanne, another Swiss town, he returned to Geneva in 1559 to help Calvin.

Calvin and Beza were very good friends and started to share many duties. Soon it was obvious that Beza could carry on Calvin's work after his death. Beza collected all of Calvin's letters and wrote a book on his life.

Theodore Beza (1519–1605)

CHAPTER SIX

A Steady Course in Adversities

We do not know much about Calvin's family life because he did not write much about himself. We know that he and Idelette had at least one child together, named Jacques, who was born prematurely and died. Calvin wrote that his death felt like a deep and painful wound. "But [God] is our Father," he said. "He knows what is best for His children."

In those days, children were seen as a sign of God's blessing and the lack of children as a curse. When someone wrote Calvin and told him that he never had children of his own because he was cursed from God, he replied, "The Lord gave me a little son and then He took him away…. In the kingdom of Christ I have ten thousand children."

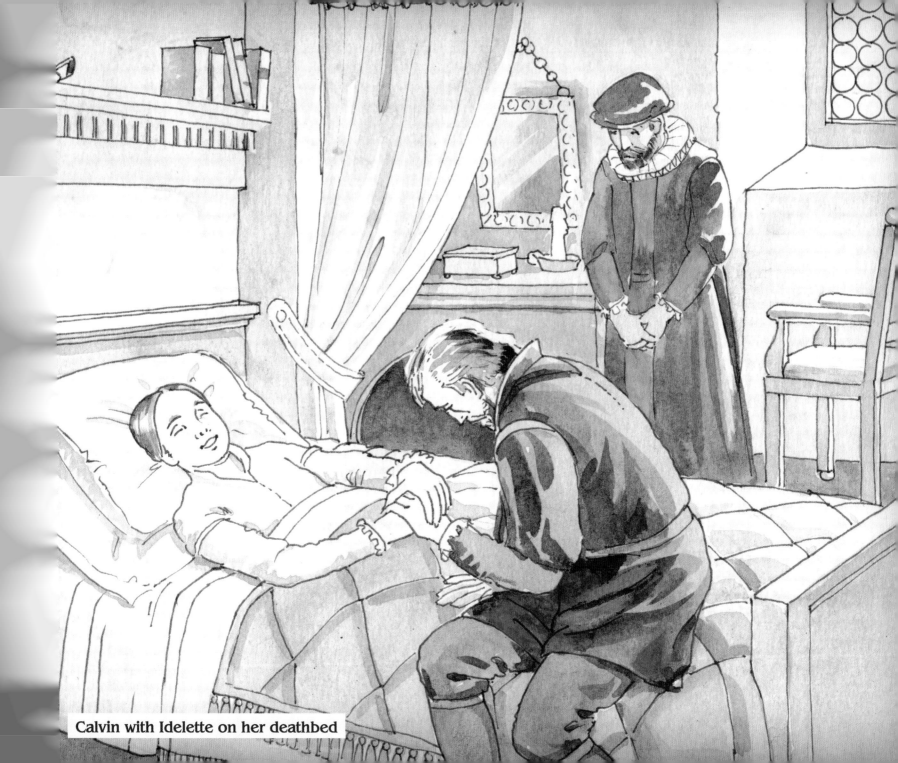

Calvin with Idelette on her deathbed

Idelette herself died on March 29, 1549, after a long illness. Calvin stayed with her until the end, assuring her that he would always continue to take care of the children that she had during her first marriage. It was a very difficult time for Calvin, whose letters describe his deep sadness and great love for his wife. In a letter to his friend Pierre Viret, he said, "I have lost the best companion of my life." Viret could understand well, because he had lost his own wife three years earlier.

Calvin continued to remember Idelette in many of his writings over the following years, and decided never to marry again. "I have now willingly chosen to live a solitary life," he said.

Calvin's life was difficult in other ways too. Besides the death of his loved ones and the many enemies that he still had to face almost daily, he suffered from very poor health for most of his life. That is why he looks so different when we compare portraits taken when he was young and others taken during the last years of his life, when he looked like skin and bones.

Young Calvin

Old Calvin

Calvin suffered from many different illnesses, some of them very serious and painful. They made his life very difficult. Tuberculosis, for example, gives terrible chest pains and makes a person cough up blood. Can you imagine preaching to a crowd of people without a microphone when you have tuberculosis? Calvin wrote about his illnesses in different letters to his friends. Around the end of his life, he spoke of high fevers and night sweats. Just before his death, he was so weak that he had to be carried to the pulpit in his chair! In spite of all this, he kept speaking of a life lived for the glory of God. When Calvin was not too sick, he exercised every day, walking for about a half hour in his room or garden, and sometimes played a game of "quoits" (similar to a game of horseshoes) with his close friends. Nevertheless, most of the time he just worked; sometimes he was even too busy to eat. For many years, he ate only one meal a day and his doctor advised him to have at least one egg and a glass of wine for lunch.

Calvin's chair

Photo by Nauticashades, Wikimedia Commons

"What? Do you want the Lord to find me idle when He comes?"

Calvin's friends were often worried about his health. He never seemed to stop working. When he was too sick to get up, he dictated to a helper from his bed. As his health became worse, his friends suggested that he should stop working and just rest. The idea sounded very strange to Calvin, who replied, "What? Do you want the Lord to find me idle [doing nothing] when He comes?"

By the end of his life, Calvin had written commentaries on almost every book of the Bible in Latin or French, three catechisms, many theological documents, and at least 4,271 letters to friends, kings, pastors, and others who wrote to him. He also personally counseled many people who traveled long distances to ask for his advice.

Some of Calvin's writings show a great sense of humor. In his day, authors often used humor when they wanted to show that something did not make any sense. Calvin did just that about the use of "relics." Relics were objects that the Roman Catholic Church considered holy just because someone said that they belonged to a famous saint.

Most Roman Catholic churches in those days had some type of "relic." Some claimed to have a part of the body of some dead saint. Calvin, however, noticed that if you counted all the different parts of the bodies that the churches claimed to have, each apostle must have had more than four bodies and each saint at least two or three! Calvin said that so many churches claimed that they had a piece of the cross on which Christ was crucified that, if it were true, the cross must have been as big as a whole shipload of timber. Yet, both Jesus and Simon were able to carry it!

Calvin's comments are very clear and humorous, and you can read them in his *Treatise on Relics*.

If all the pieces of Christ's cross that the churches were said to have were real, the cross would have been as big as a whole shipload of timber.

Calvin being carried on his chair

CHAPTER SEVEN

Last Days

On February 6, 1564, Calvin preached his last sermon in St. Peter's Cathedral in Geneva. In fact, he could not even finish it. His cough was so violent and persistent that he had to leave the pulpit. He knew then that his death was near. The following Sunday, he was carried to church in his chair to hear Beza preach in his place.

Calvin spent his last days making sure that all his jobs were passed on to someone else. He wrote letters to his friends who lived in other places, but most of the time he did not even mention his death. He just wanted to encourage them to keep the faith.

He said good-bye, however, to his good friend William Farel. "Don't get tired trying to come to me. I am already breathing with difficulty, and expect every hour that my breath will stop completely," he wrote.

However, Farel, who was then seventy-five years old, went to visit him anyway, traveling over seventy miles to spend a few last moments with his old friend.

Since Calvin had always been poor—mostly because of his generosity to others —he did not have many material possessions to leave behind. He left a silver cup to his brother Antoine, who lived in the same town, and left what little money he had to Antoine's family and other relatives.

No one in Geneva would have been surprised. Everyone knew that Calvin never cared about riches. The leaders of the Roman Catholic Church, on the contrary, had lots of money, palaces, and fancy clothes.

Cardinal Sadoleto, who had tried to convince the Genevans to return to the Roman Catholic Church, had been shocked during a visit in disguise, to see Calvin living in a small, simple house, without a servant to answer the door for him!

Even Pope Pius IV, the pope of that day, when he heard of Calvin's death, recognized that Calvin had been a strong leader because "money never had the slightest charm for him."

To the church ministers who came to see him on his deathbed, Calvin said, "My faults have always displeased me.… I pray you, forgive me the evil, and if there was any good, make it an example."

Calvin died peacefully on the evening of May 27, 1564. He was almost fifty-five years old. The funeral was held the next day, and a great procession followed his coffin to the cemetery, just outside the city.

In his will, Calvin had written that he did not want any stone to mark his grave, and no words written. He did not want his tomb to become a monument. Today, no one knows where Calvin was buried.

Calvin's deathbed

However, other monuments were built. On the 400th anniversary of Calvin's birth, the University of Geneva, founded by Calvin, built a large wall right into the old walls of the town. At the center, we see a statue of Calvin standing next to other great Reformers like William Farel, Theodore Beza, and John Knox. Under the statues, the city's motto is written in Latin: *Post tenebras lux,* which means, "After darkness, light."

Calvin left a large quantity of writings about the Bible and what it teaches, as well as a great example of devotion to God and His church. He was the first to give a well-organized explanation of what the Reformers believed and how the church was supposed to be run.

As a writer, Calvin was clear and precise. He never guessed about the meaning of any part of the Bible. If he were not sure about something, he would not write about it. Because of this, his writings are still appreciated and studied by many people today.

Calvin's ideas also helped in the development of many nations of the world. Because he taught that any job should be done as a calling from God, he inspired people to work hard and well. In addition, because he taught that the church should not be governed by the state, or the state by the church, he inspired the drafting of civil constitutions. President John Adams wrote, "Let not Geneva be forgotten or despised. Religious liberty owes it most respect."

Soon you will be ready to read Calvin's writings by yourself. A good way to start is by reading a daily devotional by him. Ask your parents to help you find one, (or get *365 Days with Calvin,* edited by Joel Beeke, and published by Day One). Above all, ask God to make you a true child of the Reformation.

The Reformation Wall in Geneva

Time Line of Calvin's Life

1509	Calvin was born in Noyon, France on July 10.
1521 or 1522	Calvin goes to Paris to study.
1528	Calvin goes to Orleans and then Bourges to study law.
1531	Calvin's father dies. Calvin returns to Paris.
1533	Nicholas Cop gives an important speech. Calvin leaves Paris.
1534	"Affair of the Placards" (posters). Calvin leaves France.
1536	First edition of Calvin's *Institutes of the Christian Religion*. Calvin moves to Geneva.
1538	Calvin and Farel are banished from Geneva. Calvin goes to Strasbourg to pastor the French-speaking congregation.
1539	Geneva asks Calvin to answer a difficult letter from Cardinal Sadoleto.
1540	Calvin marries Idelette de Bure.
1541	Calvin returns to Geneva.
1549	Idelette dies.
1559	Calvin establishes the Geneva Academy.
1564	Calvin dies on May 27.

Did you know?

❧ In Calvin's day, it was rare to have large sheets of glass to cover the windows. Glassmakers had not learned that skill yet. The poor used paper dipped in oil, which made it almost clear. Richer people sometimes used a natural crystal called selenite. The windows you see in the front cover of this book were made with ends of bottles joined together with some wire, a common practice in rich homes.

❧ Only the rich could afford to eat meat regularly. Besides raising animals in their large properties, they spent a lot of time hunting as a pastime. In fact, they ate so much meat that they suffered from illnesses like gout, a very painful disease that seems to be caused by too much red meat and rich foods. The poor ate mostly bread (without salt, which was too expensive in those days), beans, vegetables, and fruit.

❧ Besides quoits (mentioned in this story), many other games were played in Calvin's days. In France, a very popular game was "jeu de paume" (game of palm), a type of tennis played without rackets, using only the palm of the hand. Soon players started to use gloves, until rackets were also introduced.

❧ Often, common people in Calvin's day lived on the second floor of small two-story houses. On the first floor, they kept some animals (cows, sheep, goats, rabbits). During the long, cold winters, the heat from the animals would rise and keep their house warm. Many people lived in just one room, which served as kitchen, living room, and bedroom.

❁ In the centuries before Calvin's day, scientists thought that diseases came not from germs outside the body, but from some imbalance inside. Sometimes, if they thought that the sick person had too much blood in his or her body, they would take some out. It was only around Calvin's time that medicine began to discover the circulation of the blood and the spread of infections. With the invention of the printing press, these new discoveries could be published and passed on to other scientists.

❁ Calvin continued to write letters to Renée, Duchess of Ferrara. Some years after Calvin's visit, Renée's faith in the Reformed teachings became so obvious to the Roman Catholic Church that

they pressured her husband to lock her in one of the towers of her palace and send her daughters to live with nuns until she repented. Every day, someone would try to convince her to deny her faith. At that difficult time of her life, Calvin sent a pastor to comfort and encourage her. Sadly, Renée gave in to the pressures and denied her faith, but later found courage again, declared what she really believed, and went back to France where she stayed faithful to the truth until her death.

❁ Before the Reformation, the text of the Bible was not divided into verses. The first Bible to be divided into chapters and verses was the Geneva Bible, an English Bible translated in Geneva and printed in 1560 by some persecuted Christians who had found refuge there. Not all Reformers liked the new division. They were afraid that people would not see the Bible as one book, but as a list of phrases. Soon, however, they realized that it was important for people to find texts quickly, so the division was kept.

❧ Persecution against Christians was so violent in France at the time of Calvin that some French students of the Geneva Academy called their graduation a "death sentence," knowing that they would return to their country and most certainly be killed.

❧ The only songs sung in the Roman Catholic Church before the Reformation were chants in Latin. The Reformers did not always agree about the use of music and singing in worship. Some thought that there should be no singing at all. Luther and his followers wrote and sung many hymns, often to the tune of popular songs. Most Reformers in Switzerland thought that only the book of Psalms could be sung in church. Calvin preferred the Psalms, but allowed the occasional singing of other hymns. One hymn in particular, "I Greet Thee, Who My Sure Redeemer Art," seems to have been written by Calvin himself. In any case, no musical instruments were used in worship.

❧ Before the Reformation, people thought that if you wanted to be a true disciple of Christ you had to leave society and live with other Christians in quiet places away from the cities. These places were called monasteries or convents. The Reformers taught that all believers are Christ's disciples wherever they are, and that every lawful job is given by God and should be done in service to Him.